Practical
Pottery

Practical Pottery

Pottery Projects and Techniques for Creating and
Selling Mugs, Cups, Plates, Bowls, and More

Jon Schmidt

CORAL GABLES

For permission requests, please contact the publisher at:
Mango Publishing Group
2850 S Douglas Road, 2nd Floor
Coral Gables, FL 33134 USA
info@mango.bz

For special orders, quantity sales, course adoptions and corporate sales, please email
the publisher at sales@mango.bz. For trade and wholesale sales, please contact Ingram
Publisher Services at customer.service@ingramcontent.com or +1.800.509.4887.

Practical Pottery: Pottery Projects and Techniques for Creating and Selling Mugs,
Cups, Plates, Bowls, and More

Library of Congress Cataloging-in-Publication number: 2020934377
ISBN: (print) 978-1-64250-222-0, (ebook) 978-1-64250-223-7
BISAC category code: CRA028000, CRAFTS & HOBBIES / Pottery & Ceramics

Printed in the United States of America

To my children.

Table of Contents

Pottery and Parenthood

Being a potter is like being a parent.

For a short time, you care for them,
You love them,
You mold them,
You guide them through their life.

There are many stages.
In the beginning things are very messy, you have to get your hands dirty.
Eventually things become routine.
Things get hot, but they almost always make it through.
Sometimes they turn out a little different than expected, but you actually love it!

And then when your time is up, they are finished.
They are ready to move on.
All you can do is hope that the shaping you did, and the vision you had for them, is enough for them to go out and live a full and happy life.
A life doing what they were meant to do…make others happy.

My hope for you is that you will discover what you love, do it forever, and have it bring joy to the world.

Introduction

Another pottery book? Does the world really need another book about ceramics and pottery?

Hold on a second. You haven't even read it yet. You know what they say: "Don't judge a book by its cover." Or, in this case, don't judge a book by its topic.

So…what is this pottery book and what makes it different?

Well I am so glad you asked…

My name is Jon Schmidt, and I am obsessed with making functional pottery that can be used on a daily basis. My family and I own three coffee shops called Mocha Monkey, and we use handmade pots for EVERYTHING! If you come get a coffee, we have twelve, sixteen, and twenty ounce mugs for you to enjoy your latte in. If you order a delicious chicken and wild rice soup, we have sixteen ounce cups and twenty ounce bowls for you to enjoy and admire. Even our tables are adorned with handmade planters and plants arranged by the local floral shop. If you like what you are using, you can buy it or find one on the shelves just like it.

My point in telling you this is not to make Mocha Monkey sound amazing (even though it is). My point is that handmade pottery can be used for everything! From cups to mugs, plates to bowls, teapots, teacups, beer steins, candle holders, and so much more! The possibilities of form, function, and finish are truly endless!

So back to this book thing… Jon, why write a book about it?

Well, the truth is that pottery and ceramics are traditionally a very complex mix of expensive equipment, complicated chemistry, and a lot of recipes that look like they might be written in a different language. There are lots of books about what's inside clay and glazes, how to make different clay and glaze, and what happens at exactly certain temperatures inside the kiln. This is NOT that book! Yes, that stuff is important, and yes you can go as deep down the rabbit hole as you want 'til you end up with a never ending chemistry lesson. I am here to tell you that you do not have to know *everything* to fall in love with clay, pottery, and making handmade art that you can use!

And while, yes, fancy electric wheels and brand-new kilns are expensive, you don't need to spend a lot of money to make a great mug (or bowl, or cup).

This book is:

- A brief introduction for beginners to pottery and ceramics
- A testament to how amazing it is to create functional pieces you can use
- A guidebook for how to think about starting to sell and distribute your pieces
- A compendium of different projects, techniques, and ideas for anyone, whether you have thrown zero pieces or 100,000

It's amazingly satisfying to drink from mugs that you crafted, to eat meals off plates that you spun on the wheel, and to see your family and friends enjoying their lives using ware that came from your hands. Every pot you make and others use is like sharing a little bit of your story.

Most importantly, everything tastes better out of handmade pottery.

My Journey into Clay

One of the most common questions I get from people is, "how did you get into clay?"

My first experience with clay was similar to many others: a high school ceramics class. I remember it very clearly. My first teacher was Mr. Dorn, the sweetest old man you'll ever meet, who cared so much about sharing his love for clay. As with many high school courses it was about fifty minutes long, which means the first ten to fifteen minutes of the class was setting up and the last ten to fifteen minutes was cleaning up. This left about twenty to twenty-five minutes to actually work in clay… not long enough. After finishing a few ceramics courses in high school, my pieces were…terrible. Yup, they were heavy, off-center, rough around the edges, and I felt the same way about ceramics as I did about lunch period: a fun way to hang out with friends and get a little messy.

After high school ended, I went to Gustavus Adolphus College in St. Peter, MN, to play basketball. I quickly met my wife, who was also a basketball player and an art major. After a year of basketball, I came to terms with the fact that I would not be playing in the NBA and that I had to see what the world had to offer outside of playing sports. Two years into my business management degree, I decided to study abroad in India on a program called Social Justice, Peace, and Development. This trip impacted my life dramatically and is what would end up leading me to ceramics.

Typically, a course like wheel-thrown ceramics was not an option for business majors because they filled up quickly with art majors. While in India, I was allowed to register for classes before the rest of the school because of an "unreliable internet connection." Knowing that I would only be able to get into a wheel-throwing class because I had the chance to register before the rest of the school, I quickly signed up to fulfill my necessary art credit. I was also lucky enough that my then girlfriend (now wife) was an art major, so she also was able to take the class with me…*Ghost*, anyone?

I returned from India with my world flipped upside down and walked into the first day of spring semester ceramics to find twelve art majors would be my classmates. *Oops*, thought the former basketball player/business major. Seeing that I didn't quite realize what I had gotten myself into, the professor (Nicole) pulled me aside after the first class and said, "Are you sure you want to take this course? This is a very difficult course; you will have to spend lots of time in the studio."

I said, "I think I can do it." Having no idea if that was actually true.

It took just a few short weeks and about twenty hours in the studio for me to realize this was something that I was going to do for a long time. This was something with extraordinary potential and which would involve constant learning. The possibilities were endless! I found myself skipping other classes to go work in the studio. I was up in the middle of the night with new ideas. I started staying in on Friday and Saturday nights to work on my latest form idea or glaze combination. I was obsessed. After I started to finish pieces, people started asking if they could buy them. The business brain of mine took over: "I love making pottery, and people want to buy pottery. There has got to be something here." The pieces selling only added to my obsession, and I knew this was something that I had to pursue. By the end of that class I had thrown and finished more pieces than anyone else in the course.

Around this same time my mom had told me about a cool little coffeehouse called Mocha Monkey in Waconia, MN. They served everything on handmade pottery and had pieces for sale lining the shelves. I visited over spring break and again my obsessions seemed to collide. A vibrant business, with handmade pottery as a staple, in a super cool community; I needed to know more! I applied for a job.

At the same time I got a job as a part-time barista, I also found my first potter's wheel and kiln. I am thankful to my parents for letting me set up a small studio in their basement, and I somehow convinced them to pay an electrician to wire the kiln. The wiring cost four times what the kiln cost. Luckily my parents could see a fire in me (pun intended), that I had no money left after buying the kiln, and that this obsession was something to be nurtured. Just like that, I had my first little studio, a wheel, a kiln, and some shelves, so I went nuts making pots.

I had also learned that the previous owners of Mocha Monkey were looking to sell the business, and again I had that obsessive feeling that this is what I was supposed to do! Even though I had no money outside of a few thousand dollars I made as a nanny (or "manny") that summer, the prior owners took a chance on me, and we figured out a way that I would take over the business by January of 2011.

That fall I was starting my senior year of college. I remember dropping off my initial down payment to buy Mocha Monkey as my dad and I left for a mountain climbing trip. We summitted Mount Rainier in Washington just a few months before I took over operations of my new business.

I took two more ceramics courses at Gustavus, an independent study course, and got a teacher's assistant position. Each taught me about mixing glazes, firing kilns, running a studio, and more. When I took over Mocha Monkey in 2011, I still had a semester left of school. That last semester I would spend two days a week in St. Peter and the rest of the time learning and running the new business. I also had the chance to make pottery using all the college's clay, glazes, and materials, and then sell it at Mocha Monkey. It doesn't get any more profitable than that.

I quickly realized there was something very special about using handmade pottery for everyday things like your cup of coffee, bowl of soup, or as plates to eat off. After a road trip to Montana where I stumbled upon a coffee shop/pottery studio, I decided to build a small studio inside the basement of Mocha Monkey and get the wheel and kiln out of my parents' house. They were thankful.

Over the next eight years this studio produced over ten thousand pieces, over $100,000 in pottery sales, and was the site of everything from the conception of my popular Minnesota Mug to the creation of over 250 mugs given to each individual guest at our wedding in 2013.

In 2018, after returning from a soul-searching road trip, I decided that I wanted to start sharing my love of pottery with the world. I created the Jonthepotter YouTube channel in February and began uploading two or more videos per week about my life as a potter and business owner. It grew slowly, and then it began to grow quickly. I became passionate about video-making, photography, and inspiring others to do what they love. Through the YouTube channel we have been able to reach people all over the world! As of 2020, we have over 138,000 subscribers and continue to grow by the day. We now have three coffee shop locations. We just finished building a new studio at our house, only a few miles from the original Mocha Monkey location. The studio was funded partially by a successful Kickstarter campaign. This new studio has a separate kiln room, double the space of the old one, great windows, and is an overall huge improvement over the Mocha Monkey studio. My family is growing too, with two young boys, Ryder and Rory, who get to spend plenty of time in the studio.

Over the last ten years, many things have changed. I bought a business, opened two additional locations, built three different studios, got married, bought a house, a dog, a car, and had two kids, but one thing has remained consistent: I have not spent more than a few weeks at a time away from clay. If I am around a studio, I am working with clay every single day. It is something that I love. I love creating, I love trying new things. Outside of God, my wife, and my family, clay has been the most consistent thing in my life, and I am excited to share that love with you.

Since my YouTube channel started, I have professed that my goal is to instruct, inspire, and entertain. That is what I hope to do in the following pages.

For the love of clay…

Why I Love Pottery

I sometimes sit and think about why I love creating pottery so much.

For all the things in the world for me to end up doing, working with clay seemed so unlikely. My mom tells me that when I was young, I always had stuff in my hands, was always building and making things.

As a grew up, I was never good at painting or drawing; I never saw myself as an artist or even as creative. Even my first ever pottery class was just something that was fun, but nothing earth shattering. Everything changed when I got to experience the joy and freedom of unlimited time in the studio, when I started to realize that I could take a shape, form, or finish from my head, and with my hands and a spinning wheel, make something that was both beautiful and functional. The satisfaction of taking nothing but mud from the ground and ending up with a dish or a mug is something that never ceases to amaze me.

Now, after making and selling tens of thousands of pieces to people all over the world, it is intoxicating knowing that people everywhere are going through life enjoying and using pots that were crafted by my hands.

The ceramic process is just that, a process.

It isn't like painting or other art forms where if you want to change something you can see the changes in front of you. The glazed pots going into the kiln bear almost no resemblance to what will come out after it's been in a blistering two-thousand-degree environment.

The process of clay is long, and full of areas along the way that can go wrong. It can be frustrating and difficult when things go wrong for no apparent reason, but when things come out as intended, it is that much more amazing because of the misfortunes.

I heard someone say once that the ceramic process is like "slow magic." I think that's one of the best ways to put it. Ending up with a finished piece is nothing short of magical, but it is a slow process and it happens over many nights and days. Consistency and commitment are two words that come to mind when thinking about what is necessary to be successful in clay.

I guess what I am trying to express is that my love of working with mud is not insane. It may not cure cancer or end climate change, but I do believe that when people are doing what they love and what gets them excited, great things can happen.

One of the best things about pottery for me is that it seems like there are endless possibilities. Everything from the clay, to the bisque firing, to the glazing, to the firing technique and the finishing of the piece can all be manipulated in countless different ways. One can spend a lifetime in clay and not explore all the amazing possibilities. I have spent over ten years in clay, and the more I learn the more I realize how much more there is to experiment with. Working with clay is not like working with other art mediums. It takes patience, testing, an ability to endure failure, and most of all, it takes time. To become proficient on the wheel takes time. To load a kiln and fire the clay takes time. Allowing the pots to dry enough so that they will not blow up takes time. Each part of the process takes time: hours, days, months, or even years. You cannot pull an all-nighter to get work done for a show tomorrow or this weekend. You cannot get a custom set of mugs done for the local brewery in the next few days. Thought, planning, and care must go into building a sustainable pottery business that can keep up with demand while also consistently turning over inventory.

Everyone can use ceramics. Pottery and ceramics can be used in almost every scenario and business. Not only eating and drinking, but home décor, wall decorations, dog bowls, teapots, and more; there is room for ceramic art to enhance any space.

The kiln is your biggest asset. The reason that ceramics can be a viable craft and art form is because of the kiln. Mud does not hold liquid unless it is fired at over two thousand degrees Fahrenheit. Glazes look dull and boring until they get to blistering hot temperatures and come out colorful and stunning. The kiln and the atmosphere of firing take mud from something anyone can dig up out of the ground and turn it into a brilliant, functional piece that can make someone's day or year!

Why Handmade Matters

I'm sitting here drinking coffee out of a handmade mug. This particular pot is not one that I created, it's actually from one of my friends and inspirations, Joel Cherrico at Cherrico Pottery.

I am left to ponder why everything tastes better out of handmade pottery. Why is it that I notice a significant difference in my enjoyment when I get to sip my coffee out of a handmade piece of art (and not the metal travel mug I am forced to drink from occasionally)? Is it the feel of the outside, letting through just enough heat so that you know the vessel holds a warm beverage, but not enough to scald the hand? Is it because I can see the handle was cracking off the mug and that there are clearly flaws throughout the pot, but still it holds together as if it is perfect? Is it because I know and respect the hand that crafted this piece? Is it because I know someone has spent hours upon hours perfecting the craft of making this mug just so that one day I would be sitting enjoying my daily coffee out of it? The answer to all these questions and more is YES! What makes functional pottery so significant is that it is one of kind, it is unique, it was made by a person just like you and me. And just like you and me, it has imperfections, it has flaws, and for that reason it is irreplaceable.

It was not created in a factory, by machines or robots. It was not made to be as inexpensive and easy to mass produce as possible. This mug was produced because someone wanted to make it and put a small piece of themselves out into the world. It is the personal connection that you can have with a ceramic artist while you use their work that draws people to handmade ceramics and pottery!

What Do Potters Need, Both Tangible and Intangible?

Tangible

Clay

Tools (check out the tool sections for specifics)

Wheel

Kiln

Workspace

Storage/shelves

Glazes/finishes

Intangible

Grit—the ability to continue to create through failure

Consistency

A brand and/or following

Distribution channels (places to go with finished pieces)

The ability to produce enough so that there is not any attachment to individual pieces

Ten Steps to Becoming a Potter

Everyone has a different story. What will yours be?

1. Have an interest.

2. Take a class.

3. Watch the Jonthepotter YouTube channel and read this book.

4. Explore other artists' forms and functions.

5. Explore options for apprenticeships or becoming a studio assistant.

6. Explore outlets for pottery. (What will you do when you produce twenty or more pots per week? How will you sell or distribute?)

7. Explore studio options. (Garage? Basement?)

8. Buy a wheel and kiln.

9. Explore and create your own individual style.

10. Make and sell pots.

Common Clay Weight for Different Pieces

Keep in mind this can vary wildly on different levels of skill and ability, as well as on the desired thickness and finish on the piece.

	Extra Small	Small	Medium	Large	Extra Large
Mug/Cup (Approximate volume)	½ lb. (8oz.)	¾ lb. (12 oz.)	1 lb. (16 oz.)	1 ¼ lbs. (20 oz)	1 ½ lbs. (24 oz.)
Bowl	½ lb.	¾ lb.	1–2 lbs.	3–4 lbs.	5+ lbs.
Plates	¾ lb.	1 ½ lbs.	2–3 lbs.	3 ½–4 ½ lbs.	5+ lbs.
Vase	¾ lb.	1 ½ lbs.	2–3 lbs.	3 ½–4 ½ lbs.	5+ lbs.

Pottery Basics

Pottery in its most basic form is taking clay (mud from the ground) and forming it into different shapes or vessels. It is then dried and fired up to a high temperature, anywhere from one thousand degrees Fahrenheit up to twenty-five hundred degrees Fahrenheit (this depends on the clay and desired aesthetic). The firing process does a few things. First, as the clay heats up, the form that it is in becomes more durable so it will hold its shape and be more tolerant to breakage. Second, the clay begins to vitrify, which means that it will become less porous and be able to house liquid without leaking. Lastly, the firing process provides the opportunity for wonderful finishes, everything from vibrant blues and greens in electric kilns to flashes of reds and browns in wood kilns or raku kilns.

A very common process for pottery, and the one we will focus primarily on in this book, is bisque firing followed by glaze firing. Keep in mind there is massive variation in all steps of pottery making, depending on the artist and desired result. The following has been considered a simple, common, consistent process with great results for many years.

Step One: Wedge the clay. Wedging clay is the act of kneading or working the clay so it is ready to be thrown on the wheel.

Step Two: Throw anywhere from one half pound to over five pounds of clay. Throwing on the wheel is a great way to start, although hand-building pieces using slabs or coils, or by making pinch pots, are also options.

Step Three: The pots are wet from throwing and need to be dried until they get to a more workable state…"Leather hard" is a term for when the pots can be handled and still hold their shape. This can take as little as two to three hours or up to over twelve hours depending on the drying conditions. If there is air moving or if it is a dry environment this will speed up the drying time. Similarly, in a humid and still environment, it may take much longer to dry. Greenware is the term given to clay pots before they have been fired.

Step Four: Greenware pots are trimmed or altered at or slightly before the leather-hard stage. This is when we would add a handle or custom logo and finish the base of the piece before leaving the pot to dry completely.

Step Five: When the pots are finished, they are left out to get to bone dry and loaded into a bisque kiln. This state is the most fragile in the entire process.

Bisque (pronounced _bisk_): To bisque pottery means to fire clay for the first time. This firing is typically done at a temperature of Cone 06 to Cone 04 (see the cone chart later in the chapter), or between 1828°F to 1945°F.

When the firing is completed the pieces are referred to as bisqueware.

Step Six: Glazing. The pottery has now been fired one time and is in the bisqueware state. Glazes, underglazes, and different finishes can be applied before loading the pieces into another kiln and firing for a second time. This is referred to as the glaze firing

Step Seven: Unload the glaze kiln and bask in the glory of your work!

Step Eight: Figure out different avenues to sell or distribute your work so that you can keep creating new pots! There is nothing more motivating than when you are able to spark joy and happiness through your pieces being a part of people's lives!

Cone Chart

There's a full Cone Chart in back of the book!

Ceramics is often measured in "Cones." Common temperatures are as follows:

Bisque Temperatures

Cone 06 – 1828°F

Cone 05 = 1888°F

Cone 04 = 1945°F

Mid-to-High Fire Temperatures

Cone 5 = 2167°F
Cone 6 = 2232°F
Cone 10 = 2345°F

Mugs

Mugs are the bread and butter of many potters' collections. Most potters that I have talked to will say that mugs are their bestseller. I have definitely found this to be true. Why are mugs the most popular item from a potter? Short answer: I don't know. Long answer: the handle on mugs provides an additional functional and aesthetic detail. Mugs are something that many people use daily, either for morning coffee, afternoon tea, or their evening beer. Mugs are a nice price point for people, and they can usually be sold for more than a cup but less than a larger piece. People feel as if a mug with a handle is far superior to a cup. Every year I think, "Don't people have enough mugs?" Then I look in my own house, where I have far too many for the shelf and I realize the truth: You can never have too many mugs.

Form

The shape of the mug should reflect the intended use. Do you drink twenty ounces of coffee in one cup or is it better to have a five ounce cup that you can fill with coffee four different times to keep it fresh and hot? Is the mug made to show off latte art from an espresso machine which would require a shallow, bowl-like mug with a wide top? Does the consumer also like to hold the mug by the shape/form, in which case is the form conducive to a hand inside the handle?

Handle

Is the handle meant for one finger, two fingers, or the entire hand? Is the handle thicker on the top than the bottom for added strength? Does the weight of the handle, thick or thin, provide a feeling of security when drinking out of the mug?

Many of the answers to these questions are subjective and depend on who is using the piece. I find that as long as the handle aesthetically matches the shape and size of the form and is sturdy enough to hold the cup plus liquid inside, you can get very creative with handles, testing out what you like best from a handle.

Tools

There is no shortage of available tools for ceramics and pottery. From sponges, to wood tools, to knives, stamps, and more, it's possible to fill your studio with tools you never use. I know this because I have a studio full of tools I never use. In the photos that follow, I've laid out some of the most common tools for people starting out in pottery. You can decide for yourself how many of these tools are necessary for your work. While tools can enhance your work and make for an easier time, an overuse of tools can also be a burden. Keep in mind when collecting your tools, sometimes the hands and maybe one or two well-designed tools can be all that is necessary for a perfect pot.

This is a list of some of the common tools found in a pottery studio.

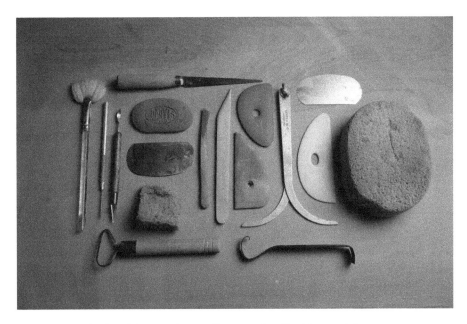

Brush—Used for brushing on glazes, slips, or other liquid materials.
Needle tool—Used for a variety of cutting techniques.
Knife and shaping tool—Used to cut, shape, and finish.
Throwing sponge—Used for efficient throwing on the wheel.

Fettling knife—Used to cut handles, slabs, and pieces of clay.

Metal rib—Used to shape, scrape, and smooth pieces.

Plastic rib—Used to manipulate shape, scrape, and smooth.

Wood rib—Used to help shape pieces on the wheel with a stiff, straight edge.

Calipers—Used for consistent measurement.

Trimming tools—Used to trim leather-hard pieces.

Serrated metal rib—Used for scoring and texturing clay.

Cleanup sponge—Used for easy cleaning and to absorb large amounts of water.

Scale—Used to weigh clay.

Wire tool—Used to cut pieces of clay as well as wire off pieces from a wheel head or batts.

Bats—Used so that pieces can be easily removed from wheel.

Heat gun or torch—Can be used to quickly dry clay or glaze.

Drill with paint mixer—Used to quickly mix up glazes.

Cookie cutters—Used to make shapes of clay from slabs.

Carving tools—Used to carve pieces.

Stamps and texturing tools—Used to make particular designs and textures in slabs or pieces.

Kilns

Kilns come in many different shapes, sizes, and fuel types. They all have different advantages and disadvantages. Since this book is primarily for the beginner who probably has never owned a kiln before, I will discuss a few different types of kilns and how they might be used.

Reduction and Oxidation Firing

There are two different firing atmospheres in ceramics and pottery. Reduction firing is when there is limited or no oxygen during certain points of the firing. Oxidation firing, which is more common, is when there is oxygen present in the firing. Many kilns can produce reduction atmospheres, although it is common for electric kilns to only fire with oxygen.

Electric

The most common type of kiln for the hobbyist/home potter is an electric kiln. These kilns typically hook up to 240-volt power, and heat is distributed through elements. An electrician should be consulted before plugging in and firing any electric kiln. These kilns are likely to fire predictably and consistently. They should be well vented, as firing any type of kiln can create potentially harmful fumes. Electric kilns are great for hobbyist potters, schools, and production potters, as they are relatively inexpensive, easy to operate, easy to maintain, and can be put in a variety of different spaces. Electric kilns are most often used for oxidation firing. Reduction firing can be bad for electric kilns and the elements. This is why most often reduction (firing with little to no oxygen) is better for gas, wood, and other types of kilns. Electric kilns are great for mid-to-high-firing ranges, such as up to Cones 6 to 8. Higher firing temperatures such as Cones 9 to over 10 are typically seen in other kilns such as gas or wood.

Bisque Kiln loaded

Gas

Gas kilns use propane or natural gas as fuel for the firing. Since there are no electrical elements, gas kilns are a great option for reduction firings. A reduction atmosphere can give clay and glaze desirable effects that are not found in oxidation firings. The lack of electrical elements also means that firing to higher temperatures such as Cones 9 to over 10 is not an issue. Typically, gas as fuel is more cost effective than electrical heat, although when kilns are full, firing expenses are relatively low regardless of the firing type.

Photo Credit: Hammerly Ceramics

Wood

Wood kilns use burning wood as fuel for the firing. The smoke, ash, and flame from the burning wood can create amazing colors and textures not found in other types of kilns. Wood kilns are great for very high temperatures (Cones 10 and over) and can produce unpredictable but breathtaking results. These types of kilns are very labor intensive, requiring constant attention and stoking of the flame. Many wood kilns are fired only a handful of times a year or less, because the process can be so grueling and it can take months of work to fill it. Depending on the size, wood-fire kilns can take many days or weeks to get to the desired temperature and cool back down to where it can be unloaded.

Photo Credit: Matthew Kelly

Raku

Raku is a process that involves firing pottery very quickly and at a relatively low temperature (Cones 04 to 06). It can produce nonfunctional, vibrant decorative finishes on pieces. While the pots are still hot they are unloaded from the kiln and put into containers with combustible material such as newspaper, straw, or hay. The pots are hot enough to ignite everything in the containers. The containers can then be closed to force the pots into a reduction atmosphere. Raku results are often unpredictable but can become consistent with time and experience. The entire process is often done in ninety minutes or less, making this one of the quickest ways to finish pottery.

Setting Up a Studio— A Space to Create

After you have taken a few classes, worked in other studios, or decided it's time for you to have your own space, there are some key things to think about. Studios come in all shapes and sizes: garages, basements, corners, barns, retail shops, anything can be turned into a space to create!

Things to Think About When Creating a Studio

Workflow: Think about your studio flow with the life of the clay in mind. Clay is brought in from the outside, it is then formed and shaped until it is dry and initially bisque fired. After the bisque fire, it is glazed and then loaded back into the kiln before eventually being unloaded, finished, and sent out to live its life. Setting up the studio strategically to align your movements with this flow can lead to better efficiency and ensure as little waste as possible. Think about the steps in your process, the flow of the clay, and let that guide you in setting up the most efficient studio possible.

Wheel: The wheel is a key piece of equipment in the studio, as it is where many projects start. When deciding where to put the wheel, it is important to think about your process. Where will the clay be stored so access is easy? Where will the pots go after throwing? Will the pots be put back on the wheel for trimming?

Kiln: Although not necessary, when possible it is preferred for the kiln to have its own separate space. This is mostly due to the fumes and the heat that are created when kilns are firing. The fumes also need to be vented, so access to the outside is a necessity wherever the kiln is being set up. Check with your kiln manufacturer, local clay store, or HVAC company to make sure that your kiln will be properly vented. This is both for better quality of firing and for safety.

Workspace/wedging table: Having a large, well-lit workspace is one of the most important parts of any studio. Besides being on the wheel, your worktable will be where you spend a majority of time. My current studio has a large four-foot-by-eight-foot table, with a piece of unfinished birch plywood as the top. This table also acts as a wedging table. In the past, I have had many different worktable tops, from stainless steel, to canvas, to concrete, and I find that the birch tabletop has been the best and all around most cost effective solution. Clay will not stick to it, making wedging easy. It does not trap and collect dust as the canvas top does. It cleans up quickly and easily, and it is easy to move and replace, unlike a large concrete-top table. My studio also has some stainless-steel tables for a glazing and extra workspace as well.

Shelving: I have found that you can never have enough shelves in a pottery studio. The more shelves I have, the more pottery I make! In my current studio, I built a shelving unit that has ware boards that slide in and out. This allows pottery to be created on the board, and batches of pots can easily be moved around from the worktable to the shelves to dry, and to the kilns to be fired. I also have shelves on wheels to be easily moved around depending on the project. Removable shelves and shelves on wheels provide flexibility in the process. Flexibility in shelving is key in a pottery studio, as pots and projects take many different shapes, sizes, and can involve differing quantities.

Storage: Having adequate storage for clay, glazes, tools, packing material, and whatever else you may need for you specific studio is imperative. Keep in mind that glazes and clay should be kept in livable temperatures so that working with them remains easy. Breaking up ice chunks in glazes makes life difficult in the winter, so make sure that you're using a temperature-controlled area.

Sink or access to water: It is important to have easy access to water as cleanup should be frequent. Clay and chemicals used in the process will clog up pipes over time, so some sort of sink trap should be installed so remnants don't go down the drain.

Other Miscellaneous Equipment

Every artist's process is a little different. Think about what other equipment you might need that would take up space in the studio.

Slab roller: Makes perfect slabs quick and easy!

Extruder: Extruders make handles, coils, and different shapes of clay very easily. Extruders can be mounted on the wall, table, or can just be handheld.

Spray booth: Many potters will spray on glazes. If this method is for you, it is recommended to have a vented booth that you can spray the glazes in.

Pug mill: A pug mill makes recycling clay much easier. It can also help to save your back and wrists from hours and hours of wedging.

Desk for office work: My studio has an area for working on the computer and doing administrative work. Many potters would choose to have this area elsewhere.

Packing and shipping: I have also set my studio up to easily turn into a packing and shipping center. Boxes, packing material, tape, and other packing supplies can be used to ship pottery from the studio throughout the world.

Mop and mop bucket: The dangers of clay dust are real. One of the best ways to prevent clay dust in the studio is to regularly mop the floors. Easy access to a mop and bucket, as well as easily cleanable floors, can make this a quick and efficient chore.

Clay

Clay is just mud from the ground. When it is heated up to different temperatures, it begins to melt and will vitrify. Vitrification means that the particles are melted close together and begin to fuse. As the clay gets vitrified the absorption rate goes down which means the clay will get to a point where it does not absorb liquid. Different types of clay have different temperatures at which they will vitrify. Earthenware clay is a lower-temperature clay. Stoneware is a mid- to high-fire clay. Porcelain is typically a high-fire clay.

Talk with your clay and glaze manufacturer about what you are looking for in a clay body. I prefer a stoneware that vitrifies around Cone 6. It is important that your clay body and your glazes match in firing temperature range. For beginners, porcelain can be difficult and frustrating to work with, and earthenware can be lower fire than would be typical for dinnerware glaze firing, which is around Cone 6. This leaves stoneware, which is widely used among schools and potters making functional work.

Many commercial clays are a mixture of different types of clays and chemicals. It is difficult to point new potters in a specific direction because there are a lot of different types of clays, and for the most part they all work very well. I would say ask your local clay supplier about a stoneware clay that can go up to Cone 6 and start there. Experiment with different types of clays to see what color, look, and feel you like best. Glazes can look very different on different types of clay bodies, so make sure you are always testing!

Wedging Clay

Wedging clay is the act of getting the clay moving. It is similar to kneading dough. Through the act of wedging, we remove air bubbles and end with a homogenous mass. Basically, that just means that the clay will be more consistent throughout all its parts and will be easier to throw on the wheel. Learning to wedge properly is an important skill to master. If done incorrectly, more air bubbles can be added to the clay. There are multiple ways to wedge but the easiest method is the ram's head method.

Start with arms bent at the top of the clay.

Starting with your shoulders, extend your arms so that the base of your palms are compressing the clay into itself

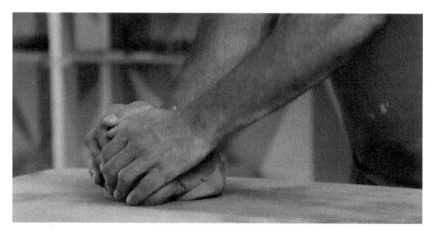

Roll the clay backward with your fingertips, so that you are now compressing a different part of the clay.

Repeat over and over until you feel the clay is properly homogenized.

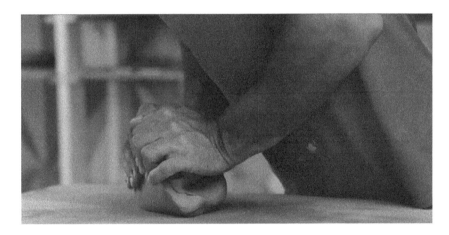

Typically, smaller pieces of clay will need less wedging, and larger pieces of clay will need to be wedged more thoroughly.

I have found that with one pound or less of fresh clay, right out of the bag, it is not always necessary to wedge. If I have more than one and a half to two pounds, I always wedge, as it makes the wheel throwing process much better.

Centering on the Wheel

Getting the hang of centering clay on the wheel is probably the single most frustrating part of pottery for beginners. You've watched satisfying videos of potters effortlessly raising up clay, magically forming vessels into unique shapes. You are sure that it can't be that hard; it looks so effortless and satisfying that you're sure throwing pots on the wheel is your calling. You sit down and spend the next thirty minutes wobbling your hands around the clay until you give up, claiming that the sorcery you've seen in videos must be edited or done by a master potter who has been throwing a thousand pots a day for a hundred years.

Centering clay on the wheel is difficult and takes a lot of time to be able to do it effortlessly and consistently. It is also probably the most important aspect of throwing, because if your piece does not start out centered, it is very difficult, and almost impossible, to have complete control over your clay.

Keys to Centering and Coning Up and Down

Start with a well-wedged ball of clay. Throw it down as close to the center as possible.

Get the clay wet with a sponge and make sure that your hands are wet. Water is necessary for centering clay quickly and efficiently. It is almost impossible to have too much water while centering. It is far more common for beginners to use too little water than too much. Later in the throwing process, it is possible to have too much water, but for the centering part, the clay and hands should be well watered.

"Coning" up and down is a common practice while centering to continue to remove air bubbles and homogenize the clay. Coning can be achieved by applying pressure with the heel of both hands at the same time from opposite sides.

As you apply pressure, the clay begins to rise in a cone shape.

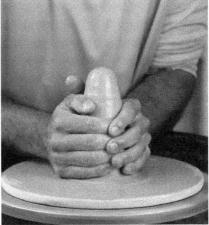

Move your hands up with the clay to complete the cone formation.

While keeping your left hand in position, and supporting from the side, slide your right hand to the top to compress the clay down into itself.

This is the position you will finish centering from, the right hand is compressing from the top while the heel of the left hand is supporting from the side.

The combination of pressure from outside and top is what will eventually center the clay. Pushing more from the top will widen the base, while slow pressure from the outside will cause the clay to become taller and skinnier.

Centering clay is done when your hands and arms are locked into a position and the clay is forced to adjust to that position. Most beginners struggle because they let the moving clay dictate where their hands go. The hands and arms must "lock" into position so that the clay has no choice but to give in.

It is important to note that being totally comfortable centering all different weights of clay takes many hours on the wheel. If centering clay does not come easily, don't get frustrated and give up. Everyone struggles to center perfectly and consistently when they first start. If you feel yourself getting frustrated, just take a little break, wedge up some new clay, and try again. You can do it; you probably just need more time on the wheel.

Cylinder: The Most Important Shape

The first assignment you will be assigned at any wheel-throwing class will be a cylinder. Why? Because most pieces you will throw on the wheel start with a cylinder, and because getting height in a cylinder can be difficult for beginners. A consistent cylinder is imperative to a potter's success. Whether you are throwing a bowl, mug, or cup, the skill to create a cylinder with consistent thickness is vital.

Start with a ball of clay.

Throw the well-formed, well-wedged ball of clay as close to the center as possible.

Make sure either the ball of clay is wet, your hands are wet, or both are. Water is key to providing the lubrication necessary to manipulate the clay while it is sliding between your hands.

Center the clay (see page 45). The wheel should be going fast.

Cone up and down.

Flatten the top while making sure the sides stay centered. Prepare the clay to create the center hole.

Create the center hole by diving in from the outer edge until you feel your fingers (or thumbs) creating a crease at the center.

Once you get to the bottom, leave enough clay for the base. It can always be trimmed later. Slowly pull the outer edge to the size you want the cylinder.

Use a sponge or hands to flatten the base.

The first pull sets the tone for the whole pot. The wheel should be slowed down for pulling. The slower the wheel goes, the slower you will pull and vice versa. If you keep the wheel spinning more quickly, you are then able to pull more quickly. Start at the base and begin to pull up the clay. The first few pulls should be more focused on getting clay up from the bottom of the pot. The top third can easily be thinned later and is commonly made too thin by beginners.

Second pull.

Third pull.

Fourth and final pull. Typically, I like to make pots with as few pulls as possible. Most small cups or mugs will be completed in three pulls. The bigger the piece, the more pulls you need to make. Beginners often need to pull many times and, as the clay gets wetter, it can get weaker and eventually fail. Don't get discouraged, it takes many pots before you feel comfortable pulling the walls.

Using a rib to straighten the sides (optional).

In most of my pots I like the throwing lines, as they provide a nice handmade touch. Ribs can be useful for shaping and finishing pots.

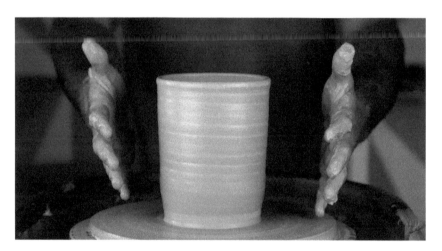

A basic cylinder.

What's Happening on the Inside?

A great habit for anyone throwing pots on the wheel is to periodically cut open your pot and check your wall thickness. It should be even across the base and all the way to the top.

This will also help us demonstrate what it looks like to pull from the inside of the cylinder.

As the photos demonstrate, your inside finger sits right on top of that outside hand all the way up until the top. The fingers can come together slightly just as we reach the lip of the pot. As a general rule, consistent, even pressure should be applied as the wheel is spinning. I find that it works well to apply the most pressure at the base of the pot where it is more difficult to get the clay up, and then slowly release pressure as your hands get to the top. While the wheel is spinning, your fingers should not move up until the wheel has gone around at least one time. This is why if the wheel is moving slowly you must pull slower.

After mastering the cylinder, you are ready to be creative with any shape that you can imagine.

Advanced project challenge: Create ten cylinders at least ten inches or taller.

Wiring off Your Pots

After throwing is complete, the clay pot needs to be separated from the wheel head or bat that the pot was thrown on. To wire off the pot, stretch the wire wide and hold it flat to the surface of the wheel or bat. Pull the wire underneath the clay while making sure you are applying downward pressure so the wire will stay as close the wheel/bat as possible. You will most likely need to wire off multiple times before removing the piece. It is common practice to wire off slowly as the wheel spins, and, if letting the piece dry on a bat, wire off again a few hours later once the piece has dried further.

Trimming

After pots have been thrown on the wheel and are dry enough to be handled, something must be done to the bottom of the pots. For beginners especially, there is often extra weight at the bottom of the pots that can be trimmed away. Trimming provides the opportunity to fashion a finished and polished base for the pot to sit on, and ensures the pot will sit flat. Depending on your style and the piece itself, trimming pots can be very simple or it can be a complex decorative feat.

When to Trim

The pot needs to be at a point where it can be handled without changing shape, but still wet enough that it can be trimmed easily. It can be tricky for beginners to judge what stage is correct. As soon as the clay is no longer sticky or wet to the touch and the lip can be handled without changing shape, it is ready to be flipped over. Once it is flipped over, the base can then dry to match the dryness of the lip. Once the base is no longer sticky and wet and is firm enough that it doesn't change shape when handled, it is then ready to be trimmed.

How to Trim

Put the pot upside down on the wheel as close to the center as possible. The first step is to get the pot re-centered. There are multiple ways to get the pot re-centered.

One way to re-center the pot is to use a needle tool on the top. Hold the needle in one spot and spin the wheel around once. Any marks made will later be trimmed away.

Wherever the needle mark is closer to the outside edge of the pot, the pot should be moved in that direction. Another way to say it is: whichever part of the pot has more clay exposed between the needle mark and the outside edge, the pot should be shifted the opposite way.

Another way to get the pot re-centered would be to use the needle tool on the outside of the pot.

Hold the needle in place and let the pot spin around. Move the needle slowly toward the pot until a mark is made on the pot. Any marks made will later be trimmed away. Stop the wheel and look where the mark is made. You can then push the pot in the opposite direction of where the mark was made. Remove the line and repeat this process until there is a small needle mark made all the way around the entire pot.

Once you feel that the pot is in the center, place pieces of clay around the pot to keep the pot from moving around. Typically, three or four small pieces of clay are enough to hold the piece in place.

You are then ready to begin trimming. Using your tool on the outside edge is a great way to start.

A common trimming technique would be to trim away from the middle and leave a small edge for the foot of the pot. Start at the middle and slowly move the trim tool toward the edge. Be careful to not take away too much as it is a common mistake to trim through the bottom.

I will typically use the tool to put an angle at the edge of the base. This gives the illusion that the pot is floating slightly on surfaces, and ensures there are no sharp edges that could scratch or be undesirable. This is also most often the place that has excess clay to be removed.

Once you are happy with your trimmed base, you can smooth out any uneven areas with your finger or a slightly damp sponge.

Mugs

Mugs, for many potters, are the bread and butter of the business. Not surprisingly, for me mugs have been my top seller since I began my pottery journey. It makes sense since I mainly sell in a coffee shop. I believe that mugs are at a perfect price point for people. They represent a vessel that gets used daily, and one can "never have too many." Mugs are often collected by people who love pottery. Other kitchen dinnerware, like cups or plates, are often found in sets. It seems that mugs can be more individual and unique. Many people don't mind having ten different mugs, but they prefer to have a set of the same twelve plates. Often you see people's favorite mug with them at the office or outside the home. Mugs can come in a huge variety of shapes and sizes. Everything from coffee and tea to beer or soup can require a different size and shape of vessel and handle.

Key Parts to a Mug

Form: The form of a mug must be aesthetically pleasing while also being functional. What will this mug be used for, what is it meant for? How much liquid should it hold? What kind of handle will it have? How will it be finished? Answering these questions will help you decide how much clay to start with and what the form should look like.

Base: The base of the mug can be trimmed after throwing or cut into the clay while still wet on the wheel. The base should be wide enough to support the weight of the mug when full of liquid. The wider the top of the mug, the more unstable it will be when filled with liquid.

Handle: Handles should be functional and add to the aesthetic of the pot. (See page 85 for the chapter on handles.)

Lip: The lip of the mug is where your pot meets its owner's mouth. It is one of the most important parts of the mug and can be made in many different ways. Some people prefer thicker lips, while others prefer more thin but fragile lips.

I make many mugs to be used at the coffee shop; they are handled hundreds of times by different people and washed over and over. I purposefully put much thicker lips on these mugs, since they are abused much more than mugs that might sit in someone's home.

Finish: Mugs can be finished in a variety of ways. It is important that they are finished in a way that is food safe, easily cleanable, and which will not leak when filled with liquid.

Mugs can be made from about a half a pound of clay for a smaller espresso style mug up to around two pounds for a larger twenty-five to thirty ounce beer stein or large coffee cup.

The Basic Steps to a Mug

1. Throw or create the form.

2. Let dry until leather-hard or slightly before leather-hard (this takes anywhere from three to twenty-four hours depending on humidity and stillness of environment).

3. Perform any trimming necessary.

4. Create handle.

5. Attach handle when dryness of form is similar to the dryness of the handle.

6. Let dry to bone dry.

7. Fire once in bisque.

8. Glaze/finish pot and fire again.

9. Drink from mug and be delighted.

Throwing Three Shapes of Mug

Cappuccino Mug

Center low and flat.

Pull out wide.

Create a basic cylinder in one or more pulls.

As you pull up, you can begin to create the bowl-like shape. More pressure can be applied with the inside hand.

Keep the lip a smooth, curved shape throughout the process.

The form can continue to be refined in the last few pulls.

Make sure you get all the excess water from the base.

Set the mug aside to dry until it is ready to trim and put a handle on.

Hourglass Shape—Wide Base and Wide Top

This shape is great for those who like to put their hand inside the handle. It fits the hand well while also providing a comfortable lip shape to drink from.

Center low and flat.

Create the center and pull out a little wider than normal.

Make sure the bottom is flat and remove excess water.

Begin to pull up, making sure to keep the base wide.

The first pull should focus on bringing the top of the cup inward. Focus on making a pyramid shape by applying more pressure with the outside hand/finger.

Begin the next few pulls in the same manner, making sure the base stays wide, but immediately forcing the outside hand to make the cone-like shape upward.

In the middle pulls you can allow the lip to start to flare out at the top. This should not be done until you feel comfortable you have most of the weight out from the base. It is always easy to flare out the top, but it is very difficult to get it to come back in.

The last pull can be the one that finalizes the hourglass shape, making sure to smooth the lip at the top. If you can't make the shape you desire by just pulling it, you can use a rib (plastic, wood, or metal) to help make the shape into what you desire.

Finished shape.

Wider Middle with a Flared Lip

This form is a great all-round shape that many people enjoy. Over the years this has become a go-to shape for me. The comfortable lip and aesthetically pleasing form make for a lovely drinking experience.

Center and create middle as normal.

First pull, you will pull up just like a straight cylinder.

For your second and subsequent pulls, you can begin to make the shape of the mug, moving the top of the cup outward.

Start to pull the shape back inward when you are about two thirds of the way up. Then flare the lip out slightly at the top. Do not do this too early, as it is easily done in later stages.

The lip can be shaped and smoothed throughout the throwing process.

The shape can be refined in the final few pulls.

You can use a plastic rib to smooth and refine the shape even further (this is optional).

Make sure the bottom is smooth and remove any excess water.

Set aside to dry before attaching the handle.

Handles— Can You Handle It?

Handles can be made in many different ways. I use an extruder to do the majority of my handles. An extruder is a large tubular piece of equipment in which a plunger pushes clay through a mold or "die." It is a very efficient way to make a lot of handles quickly and consistently. The first way that most beginners are taught to make handles is by pulling. To pull a handle you start with a piece of clay and make that into a shape that you can pull down with a wet hand. As your fingers slide down the clay you can begin to form the handle shape. This method allows for a shape that has more weight toward the top of the mug and less as it gets to the bottom. Pulling handles takes quite a bit of time and extra effort, but those that are proficient at it can create amazing handles.

Handles can also be formed from coils, slabs, as well as by using a tool to cut a handle out of a piece of clay.

Things to Think about When Creating Handles

Handles are an important part of mugs, pitches, teapots, steins, and many other vessels. The handle should be both functional and aesthetically pleasing. Handles should reflect and enhance the form where they're attached.

Size: The size of the handle should depend on the size of the vessel, how it is meant to be used, and the personal preference of its maker or users. For example, a beer stein will often have a large handle which the hand can fit completely inside, while a smaller teacup might have a more delicate handle where only one finger fits.

Shape: The shape of the handle comes down to the preference of the maker. It can often dictate how many fingers fit into the handle as well as the way in which it is held. Many people also like to hold mugs in a way that doesn't include the handle. When designing a handle, thought should be given to the ways the vessel could be held, including by using the handle and gripping the vessel.

The best way to learn about what handle you want to create is to use different mugs, pitchers, teapots, or other handled forms. Look at others' work and decide what you like and dislike about the form and function of different types of handles. Try making and using different styles of handles and you will learn a lot about what you both like and dislike. There is no one right answer about handles; many people have different opinions about why they love their favorite handles.

The Advantages of Using an Extruder

- **Efficiency:** You can create many handles with minimal effort.
- **Consistency:** You will get a consistent size and shape.
- **Durability:** The compression of clay inside the extruder adds strength and durability.

How to Make and Attach a Handle

Whether you are pulling a handle, extruding a handle, or cutting a handle from a slab, the steps to attach it are the same.

Start by scoring or scratching where the handle will be attached to the mug, both up near the lip and near the base.

Create the desired handle shape to be attached to the mug and score where it will attach.

Apply slip or liquid clay to the scored part of the handle. This will act as a bond and keep the pieces of clay attached.

You can now press the handle into the mug where you have previously scored.

I prefer to blend where the handle joins the mug to give a very smooth and cohesive look. Some potters will choose to blend less or not at all depending on the desired look.

A finished basic handle.

Other Handle Shape Examples

I always find it helpful to let the handles dry upside down to help them keep their shape.

Bowls

Bowls are one of the easiest forms for beginners to make. When you first start on the wheel, it's a very natural motion for the clay to get wider at the top than at the base. This is why it is important to start by creating tall cylinders so you learn how to properly pull up the clay and get height before you let the natural motion of the wider top take over. Bowls can be made in all shapes and sizes. You can start with anything from less than half a pound for little trinket dishes, all the way up to ten or more pounds for giant decorative bowls. For the project below we made some basic shaped bowls with around two pounds of clay. They would go well in any kitchen and could be used for soup, ice cream, cereal, pasta, salad, and more!

How to Make a Bowl

Start with a well-wedged, circular ball of clay.

Center the clay as normal. You can center lower and flat if throwing a wide, short bowl. You can center taller if you are throwing a skinnier or taller bowl.

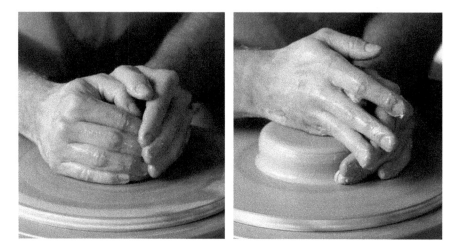

Use one or two fingers to create the center and slowly start to pull out.

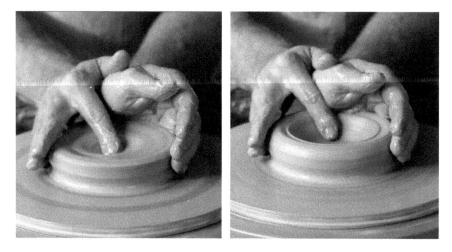

Use your fingers or a sponge to smooth out the base and create a cohesive inside shape. Keep the base flat, and, as you pull out, you can start to form the interior of the bowl.

You are now ready to pull up the sides. Start from the base and, keeping your inside hands slightly above your outside hand, pinch in and pull up the clay. Remember that you will always be able to make the top wider later, but it is much more difficult to bring it back in once it gets wide. The first few pulls are important in trying to keep that straight cylinder shape.

After the first pull (or a few), your pulls can start to reflect the bowl shape.

The last (optional) step would be to use a metal, plastic, or wood rib to help complete the shape of the bowl.

Ribs work great on the outside and help to push from the inside. The clay is forced to reflect the shape of the rib on the outside. Just like pulling the walls, use the inside hand starting from the base to slowly climb up the rib on the outside. Experiment with different shapes, types, and flexes of ribs to see what works best for you!

Plates

Plates can be one of the most temperamental shapes for potters. The flat, wide shape lends itself to warping and cracking. The larger the size, the more they should be "babied" throughout the process. This means making sure they dry evenly and consistently as well as making sure the thickness is even when throwing. Smaller plates can be made with one to two pounds of clay, while larger dinner plates would require three to four pounds of clay. For the set of eight inch plates described below, we started with just under two pounds for each plate.

How to Make a Plate

Start by centering the clay as normal, coning up and down for consistent clay.

Plates can be centered very low and flat. While providing support with the left hand, you can use the edge of the palm to create a flat top on the center piece.

Using the edge of a fist or a sponge, start from the center and consistently pull out the clay.

When you flatten the clay out to about the right size, you can begin to work on the lip of the plate.

Since plates are typically made in sets and most people want them to stack neatly, we are using calipers to measure the size of the plate.

Using your forefinger and thumb, just slightly pinch from the base of the clay to create the lip, you can "pull up" by pinching into a sponge or your other hand to create a smooth and consistent lip.

Using a rib, make the center of the plate flat and a consistent thickness. Start in the center and slowly flatten by going out toward the edge. This technique is commonly referred to as compressing the clay. This method may help prevent "s-cracks" simply because it helps to make the base thickness consistent and promotes even drying.

The Potter's Swirl

The Potter's swirl is a great technique for adding depth and interesting detail to any piece with a large flat base. Start in the center with the wheel going slow.

While applying pressure with one finger, begin to pull outward consistently at a rate slightly faster than the wheel is spinning.

The swirl will begin to form. Continue to pull outward at a consistent speed so that circles form all the way out to the edge.

Potter Efficiency Hack

I have a laser pointer set up to use if I want to throw a lot of pieces that are the same size. This way I don't have to use calipers every time I need to measure, I can just throw the plate and stop when the lip is at the laser point.

Remove the plate from the wheel head and make sure it dries very evenly. If they're big plates, I find I have the best luck if I let the plates dry very slowly over a few days or even a week.

Planters

Planters are a fun and functional project. Planters are not used for food or drink, so when glazing and finishing you can try out techniques that may not be appropriate for food ware, like raku or different specialized glazes not meant for contact with food. You can even leave the inside of planters unglazed, which helps to retain some moisture. The key aspects to planters are the drainage holes and how the drained water is caught. Most plants thrive when they have well-drained soil, which means that the planters need to have holes that will let the excess water out. I have made planters in two different ways, one with an attached drip tray and another with a separate plate to catch the water.

How to Throw a Planter with an Attached Drip Tray

Start with however much clay you need for the size plant you have. Half a pound to a pound would be good for a small succulent, while larger planters could be made with over five pounds of clay.

Center and cone up and down as normal.

Pulling up the clay from the base is where this project is different from others. Instead of starting all the way at the bottom of the clay, start pulling up from just above the base. Leave half an inch or more clay at the base that will be made into the tray after we have put in drainage holes.

Continue to pull up the clay in whatever shape you want for your planter.

Once you have the basic shape of the planter, you can put in the drainage holes. The reason we punch the holes in now is because after we throw the drip tray it is much more difficult to do.

One hole is probably enough for many planters, but for this project we put three holes, evenly spread around the pot.

We are now ready to throw the drip-tray edge that will contain the water.

You can then set the planter aside to dry until it can be flipped over and trimmed.

How to Throw a Planter with a Separate Plate as a Drip Tray

For this project we are throwing two separate pieces that will go together once they are finished. The plate that goes under the planter must be larger, but not so big that it looks like they don't go together.

Start by throwing the planter part. Center and pull up as normal in whatever size and shape you prefer.

I finished this piece in my "twisted" style. To accomplish the twisted look, take one finger from the inside, and support with two fingers on the outside. Slowly bring it up toward the top, while the wheel is also moving slowly. Let the wheel spin around until you can do the next twist. I usually get somewhere between five and eight twists done. As long as the movement is consistent, you will get a pot that looks like it is twisting.

Once the planter part is dry enough you can flip it over, trim, and put a few holes in the bottom for water to drain through.

Next you will need to throw the plate. Measure the planter part to make sure you throw the plate larger than the base of the separate pot. Center the clay low and flat.

Pull the clay to the edge just like you would for a plate.

Create the edge so that the water will remain well contained.

For this plate, I added a potter's swirl to help the water drain out easily from underneath the planter.

Berry Bowl (Strainer/Colander)

A berry bowl is a fun and useful piece that can be used to wash fruit, drain noodles, or for many other kitchen-related tasks. In its simplest form, it is basically a bowl that will hold solids but let liquid drain through. For this project, we added many holes to the piece so that draining is quick and the piece is easily identifiable. In reality you don't need an excessive number of holes. Ten to fifteen would probably do the trick, but once you start creating those holes, using them as a design element can be fun and inviting.

How to Make a Berry Bowl

Start with anywhere from two pounds of clay up to four pounds or more depending on the desired size of the piece.

Center the clay low and flat.

Create the center of the bowl by pushing down in the middle and slowly pulling out the clay until you have reached the desired size for the base of the bowl.

Begin to create your cylinder by pulling up the clay.

Continue pulling the clay until you have created a simple, consistent bowl shape. A plastic rib can be used to shape the bowl. The bowl will then be set aside to dry until it can be flipped over and trimmed.

Trim the bowl to give it the desired foot size (see page 62 for more on trimming), keeping in mind that you will be adding holes to the base and sides of the bowl for the liquid to drain.

Now you can begin to add holes in a desired pattern. I used a hole punch for this project. A straw can also work well to create clean holes. The holes can be placed randomly, spiraled, in lines, or however you can think of. The goal is just for liquid to be able to flow out while keeping larger pieces such as berries or noodles inside. It is worth noting that the holes should be big enough so that glaze will not run and plug them during the glaze firing.

The bowl can then be flipped over, and any stuck pieces of clay removed. Clean up around the edges of the holes to make sure that there are not sharp edges after the piece has been finished. You can also do this as the piece firms up even more.

The bowl can be left alone after you've finished trimming and placing the holes. I typically like to add handles to two sides for easy grabbing, lifting, and as an added aesthetic detail. For these handles I am using extruded clay.

Score and slip where the attached handles will go. (See page 85 for more on handles.)

Blend the handle into the piece for a cohesive look.

You can get creative with the handle by spiraling or adding clay to make it more decorative and functional.

Chip and Dip

The "chip and dip" bowl is one of my favorite pieces to create. It is a difficult and challenging piece, but it is a standout in any kitchen or dinner party. The uses range from holding chips and salsa, veggies and dip, or even standing in as unique planter for different kinds of succulent! These amazing pieces have always been a top seller. Whenever I find time to create these unique pieces, it is always worth it.

How to Make a Chip and Dip Bowl

Start with anywhere from three to five pounds of clay for the bigger bowl.

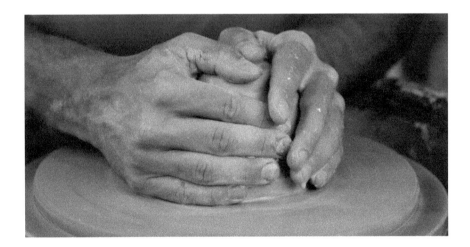

Throw the bowl as you would a normal bowl. Center, low and flat, create the cylinder, and pull until you have the desired bowl shape. (See page 93 for more on bowls.)

Once the desired shape is achieved, you are then ready to create the base for the smaller bowl to sit on. Do this by taking two hands and folding in an edge of one side of the bowl. If your clay walls are too thin or too wet, this will not work. You can wait for the sides to firm up before folding in the edge.

You now need to throw the smaller bowl. Start with anywhere from a half pound up to one and a quarter pounds of clay depending on the size of the bigger bowl and the desired size of the dip bowl. Throw a small bowl; the base should be a similar shape, so it fits nicely into the indent that you created in the larger bowl.

When you are ready to trim the smaller bowl, you can trim differently than you normally would for a bowl meant to exist on its own. For this bowl you can trim a half circle, such that it would not sit flat on a table but will fit snuggly into the indent created in the bigger bowl.

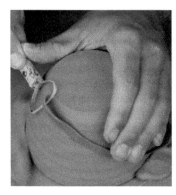 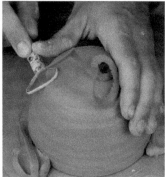 

After trimming both the bigger and smaller bowls, once they are both at a similar moisture level you are ready to attach them. Score the indented area as well as the smaller bowl. I find it helpful to hold the small bowl in place to see where it will fit best and then make marks on the bottom so that I know where to score and use slip.

Once the smaller bowl is in place, take a small coil of clay to put around all sides of the bowl. This will help to create a strong bond between the two pieces and create a cohesive look.

It is important to look at the attached bowl to make sure that it is level and not leaning one way or another. If it is fired with a slanted top bowl, the firing process it will most likely make the sagging worse. Finishing with a level bowl is vital to the success of this project.

Add a piece of clay on the outside (and inside if desired) to keep the bowl from sagging as the piece dries. Optionally, you can fire that piece of clay in the bisque fire to help ensure the bowl stays in place.

Coffee Pour Over

Some would argue that a single-cup coffee pour over is the best way to enjoy the beloved hot beverage. This piece is a simple mug design with a few added alterations. The base saucer must be big enough to fit on top of most mugs, the holes in the bottom must allow coffee to drip through at a slow consistent pace, and the top part must fit a coffee filter, while encouraging the flow of coffee. The wonderful thing about this method of coffee-making is it requires no power or equipment. All you need is hot water, ground coffee, a coffee filter, and you are ready to make a delicious hot cup of joe anywhere!

How to Make a Coffee Pour Over

Start with one to one and a half pounds of clay for a single cup. You can start with more clay if you want to experiment with a multiple cup brewing method.

Center clay as normal, but instead of pulling up the clay from the bottom, you will leave about half to three quarters of an inch of clay to form the base of the pour over.

Create the center hole as normal.

Begin to pull up the clay, making sure to leave the clay on the base.

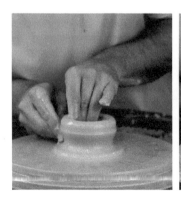  

The base can be spread out with the clay left on the bottom. It will be finished later during trimming.

Set the piece aside to dry.

After the form has had a little time to set up, you can then run a wire underneath to release it from the bat. Flip over and let the base dry until it is ready to trim.

The base then can be trimmed to the desired look, although it is important to think
about the liquid that will be coming down through the bottom of the pot. A small rim

of clay should be left after trimming. This will make it so the coffee falls down into the mug beneath it as opposed to sticking to the base of the pot and dripping outside the mug. Another method would be to trim it flat and add a small coil as a drip catcher.

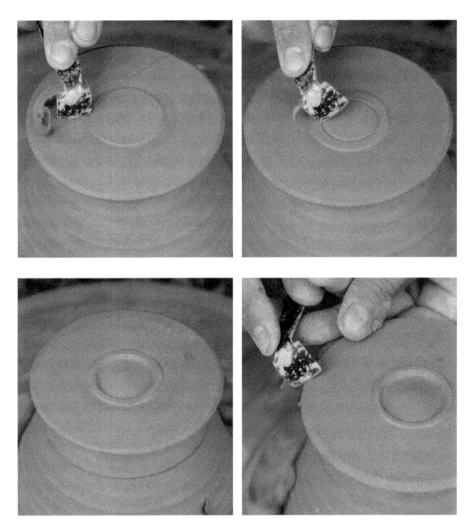

Put holes on the inside of the rim on the base. I have experimented with different shapes and sizes of holes, and, as long as they aren't too big or too small, it will usually work well. Try anywhere from one bigger hole up to eight smaller holes to see what will work the best for you and your desired coffee method.

Optionally, a handle can be added for additional functionality and aesthetics. Many potters do not bother adding a handle.

Additionally, it can increase functionality to add some sort of texture, carving, or alteration to the inside of the pour over. Filters can suction to a purely circular form, causing the coffee to struggle to flow through. Creating different forms or alterations can help the coffee flow.

Pitchers

Pitchers are great for storing larger amounts of liquid to then pour into other vessels. A large pitcher may be used to serve lemonade or tea, whereas a smaller pitcher might be used for cream or syrup. The defining quality of a pitcher is the spout. Creating a functional spout that pours easily without dripping can take a lot of trial and error.

How to Make a Pitcher

For this pitcher we started with about two and a half pounds of clay, which created a vessel that holds eight cups of liquid.

Start with a well-wedged ball of clay, and center it as you would for a normal pot.

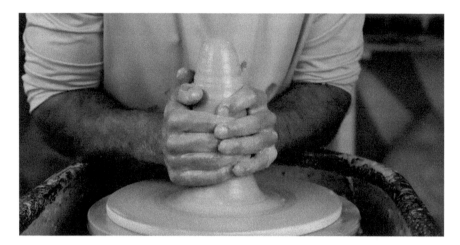

Make the hole in the center.

Pull up and focus on making a straight cylinder shape.

Once the cylinder is created, you can use a rib to form the belly or the shape of the desired pitcher.

The top lip should be flared out before the spout is made; this will help prevent drips and make the spout functional.

To create the spout, push back with two fingers and, with one finger between those, create the spout form. It is important to note that just pushing out with one finger is not enough to create a functional spout; there also needs to be two fingers pushing in toward the pot to create a funnel-like shape that the liquid can flow through.

After the spout is made, you can then let the pot dry until it is ready to put a handle on.

Score and apply slip where you want to attach the handle.

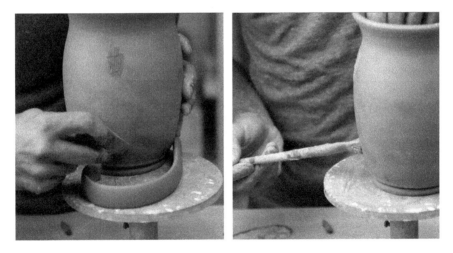

Since this is a large handle, I found it easiest to attach upside down so the handle wouldn't slump when drying.

Blend the handle together with the form and set aside to dry.

Tri Bowl

This piece is a wonderful serving dish. It can be used in a taco bar with salsa, guacamole, and cheese or as a centerpiece filled with different kinds of candy. The key to this piece is to be able to throw three bowls that are very similar sizes. Trim the bowls how you want, connect them together (adding small coils for extra strength), and lastly, add a handle for both decorative and functional purposes.

How to Make a Tri Bowl

Throw the bowl.

Center the clay low and flat, then pull up to create a small bowl.

Use the last pull or a rib to make the final bowl shape.

Using calipers or some sort of measuring device, measure the width and height of the first bowl so that you can throw two more bowls of identical size and shape.

Set aside to let dry before finishing the base.

Repeat previous steps two more times.

After throwing the three bowls, let dry until they can be flipped and their bases can be finished. (See page 62 for more information on trimming.)

Put the bowls together in the desired arrangement and mark the tops.

Mark the points of contact between the bowls so that you can score and apply slip before attaching.

Apply slip to the points of contact.

Squeeze together the areas that need to be connected.

Small coils can be added to the intersections for added strength.

Lastly, a handle can be attached for both decorative and functional purposes. We used a small piece of clay to hold up the middle of this handle so that it stays in that same spot as it dries.

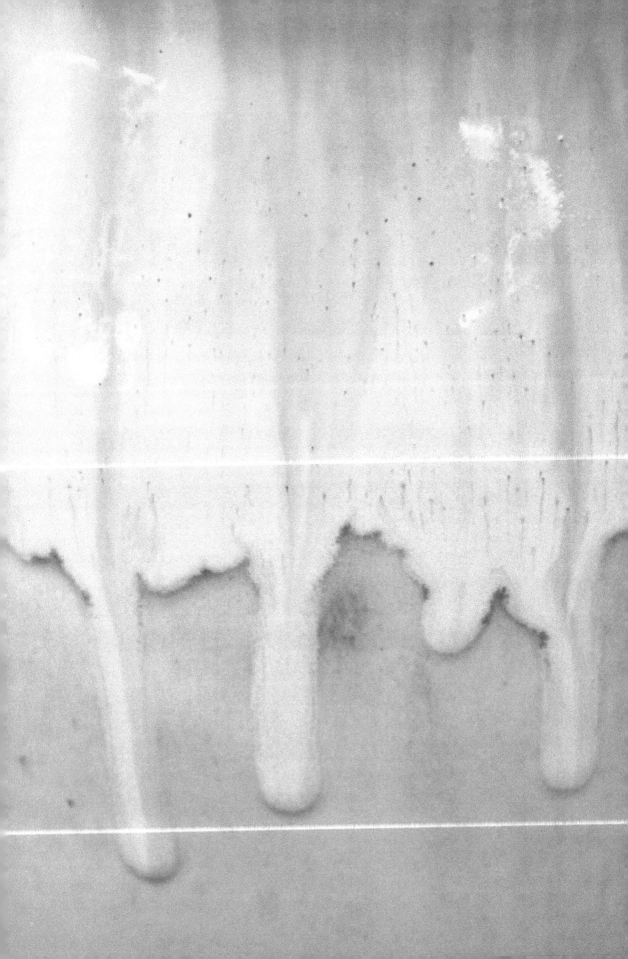

Glazing and Finishing

There seems like an infinite variety of ways to finish pottery after it has been thrown and fired. From different types of kilns to different firing temperatures, the options are endless. When deciding how to finish your pieces, it often comes down to what you have access to, your experience, and your desired finish. If the pots are to be used to hold liquid, then you should make sure that the clay is fired up to its minimum vitrification temperature. If it will be used as a decorative piece, then the vitrification is not as important, and the desired finish is the only concern.

Glaze Application

There are many different ways to apply glaze, but I will focus on just a few.

Dipping

Dipping is a common way to evenly and efficiently apply glaze to pots. Dipping is a great way to coat pots in a thick layer of glaze. It is necessary to have a larger amount of glaze to be able to dip appropriately. Five pounds of dry glaze made up in a gallon bucket is the minimum you would need to dip smaller items like cups, mugs, or bowls. Dipping and, when necessary, pouring have been my application methods of choice for many years. Dipping is an easy and efficient way to layer glaze combinations, often with stunning results.

Pouring

Pouring the glaze on to pieces is similar to dipping, as it will evenly distribute glaze around the pots. Pouring can be used when dipping is not an option, either for larger pieces or if you do not have a sufficient amount of glaze. Pouring can also be an effective way to create different designs.

Brushing

Using a brush to paint on glaze can be great if you don't have a lot of glaze or if you need to be very specific in the application. Typically, brushed-on glaze goes on much thinner than with dipping or pouring, so two to three or more coats may be necessary.

Spraying

Spraying glaze onto pots using a spray gun can be an efficient and effective way to evenly apply glazes. The spraying process will give a different appearance than other application methods. Safety precautions should be taken when spraying, as inhalation of any ceramic material can be very harmful. A vented spray booth and ventilation mask are recommended.

Using Wax Resist when Glazing

Wax is a great way to keep glaze off areas that you want to remain bare clay. The bottom of a pot is a great example. When firing a glaze kiln, any glaze that comes in contact with another surface will fuse together with it. Two pots that are glazed and set in the kiln touching each other will fuse together. A pot set in the kiln with glaze on the bottom will fuse to the kiln shelf. For this reason, you must make absolutely sure that you do not let any glaze touch areas you don't want it to. Wax resist is a great way to keep glaze from adhering to the clay. Simply paint on wax resist and let it dry. When applying the glaze later on, it will come right off the waxed areas, and the wax burns off during the firing at a relatively low temperature.

How to Dip and Pour Glazes

Make sure that your glazes are well mixed. After even just a few minutes, the glaze can begin to settle, so you want to make sure that you mix the glazes up frequently.

Using tongs is a great way to dip the entire pot.

After lifting the pot out of the glaze, you can then wipe the bottom. If you used wax resist, the glaze should come off with no problem.

Set aside to dry until you layer with more combos or further decoration.

Another way to dip is to just dip the top lip and then layer additional glazes on top.

For this pot, we want to add one additional layer of glaze on the entire interior of the bowl and a little on the rim. Start by pouring the glaze inside the pot.

Once there is enough glaze inside, you can twirl it around to coat as much as possible.

As you pour out the glaze, you can twist your hand to evenly distribute glaze around the rim.

After pouring, you can dip the lip in as far as you want covered. This will help to create an even, consistent layer of glaze around the lip and promote some glaze flow on the outside.

For the second pot, we will dip the entire pot into the second glaze and set aside to dry until we are ready to fire.

It is important to remember that the more glazes that are layered, the more the glazes will drip when fired. As a general rule, I never layer more than three different glazes when dipped and poured, and typically I only layer two or more on the top third of the pot. After testing your own glaze combinations, you can start to discover which combinations will run heavily and which ones can be layered further down on the pots.

Brushing goes on much thinner, so three coats of each glaze, for a total of six or nine coats, may be necessary to achieve the desired results.

How to Find Yourself as an Artist

When you are first starting out, finding your own individual style can be difficult. You don't quite have the skills necessary to really be proficient as a ceramic artist. Everyone starts out by looking at other artists' styles and trying to replicate them. Two common questions I get over the years are: 1) How do I find my own style? and 2) Is it okay to copy other artists? I believe that the answers to these two questions are closely related. I believe that it is okay to try to replicate other artists' work in an effort to improve yourself, continue learning new skills, and move toward finding your own style that is unique to you. When you first start you will have no idea where to go, what to do, or how to do it, among many other things. The only way to find your own style is to get inspiration from others. The problem arises when you fixate on one style or one artist and never move on to making it your own; this then becomes plagiarism. Once you are able to create pieces resembling the artist you are trying to recreate, it is then time to move on to either explore new inspirations or to work on creating something that is clearly your own.

I have been sharing my work and my process online now for many years. I have seen many people trying to replicate what I do, whether in terms of form, finish, decoration, or business model. I am totally okay with this, as I share freely so that people can learn, be inspired, and be entertained. I have also seen people who try to create a business around exactly what I am doing. It's a problem when you are trying to make money from someone else's ideas, without their permission.

If you are a beginner, I encourage you to find inspiration from other artists! Try to replicate what you see and what you enjoy, but keep searching for a style that will make you unique! Once you find that style, keep searching, because the world can always use more of what is unique.

The Business Side of Potting

Maybe you picked up this book and said, "Hey, I threw pots in high school, that was fun, maybe I could do that again." Maybe you said to yourself, "I really want to make a living as an artist... Pottery is cool!" Or maybe you just wanted to look at some pretty pictures and imagine getting your hands dirty. The fact of the matter is, if you are going to get into pottery for the long term, eventually you will have to start selling or distributing your pottery. Even if you think that it's just a hobby now, if you want to continue to get better and improve you *must* find avenues to distribute your work. You probably don't have enough family and friends to give away all the pots, and your garage probably isn't big enough to house the thousands upon thousands of pots you are going to create after reading this book! If this is something you will do for more than a few months, you can never start thinking about selling too early.

I cannot stress this enough. There is nothing more motivating for improving your skills than selling or distributing your work. On the flip side, there is nothing more demoralizing than having a bunch of pots sitting around. One of the keys to being a great potter is creating a lot of work over a long period of time and continuing to try new things. You cannot do this if every pot you make is very special to you. You must detach yourself emotionally from the outcome of the pot, so that when things don't turn out you can move on and keep trying new things! Detaching yourself also allows you to be free with your experimentation. This is why it's so important to find outlets for your pot making, so that you can keep creating and exploring. It can be difficult at first to put yourself out there, opening yourself up to criticism, but to really grow as a potter and an artist it is imperative to start thinking about the selling aspect.

It Starts with a Following

Two great myths:

Myth One: Become good at something and people will start to follow you.

The reality: People can start following you while you are still becoming good at something.

Myth Two: Gaining a large following of people happens overnight.

The reality: For most people, gaining a large following happens over a long period of time and with a lot of hard work.

For example, when I first started creating YouTube videos for the Jonthepotter YouTube channel, I had never shot or edited videos before. The first seventy to eighty videos I put up were terrible! But people started to follow what I was doing, and by video one hundred the videos were actually pretty decent, I was getting pretty fast at editing, and I was enjoying it! Over the course of a year I had learned to shoot and edit videos, and all the while people were joining in my story! After eighteen months of getting better at making videos and improving my pottery skills, we had over 131,000 subscribers and continue to grow rapidly.

It is never too early to start gaining a following. A following of people is what will help you to create and sell pots in the future, at the end of the day, followers/fans = customers. The more fans you have, the more options you have. Whether that following is in your local town or online, you need people following you to make selling easy and efficient. You may think you're not good enough to post pictures online, or to have a website, but guess what? Building a following TAKES TIME! If you start now, even if you're not good enough yet, by the time you are good enough, then maybe you will have enough of a following to be able to sell your pots.

What do people and potential customers love even more than great pottery? A great story! Start telling yours. Building a following is basically all about telling your story. By starting to tell your story NOW, you are starting to build that following for future selling.

Branding

Creating a brand is telling your story. What story are you going to tell?

The Process

Pottery is a unique, interesting, and very visually appealing process. Sharing your process with your potential followers can be a powerful part of your brand. Everyone has different ways that they work and different personalities; don't be afraid to share how messy or clean, or perfect or imperfect yours is! People love seeing others fail, so often showing your failures and hardships can actually be more effective than making yourself look great all the time!

Selling

Think about how you want to sell your pots. It is important for you to understand the pros and cons of the different ways to sell. Once you decide how you want to sell, you can then begin to put the pieces in place so that you can grow your following and brand in that area. Each way takes different skills, a different marketing strategy, and requires different efforts. Most artists usually focus on just one or two of these avenues because they take up a large percentage of time that could be spent creating pots. Over the past ten years I have acquired experience with each of these different ways of selling, giving me some insight into the pros and cons.

Friends and Family

Our first ever sale, back when we were in college, was a little family-and-friends sale at my then girlfriend's, now wife's, parents' house. We invited all our friends and extended family to see what we had been making and gave them a chance to buy. They LOVED it! People bought lots of terrible pots; at the time I thought they were great, but looking back now I know that I had a long way to go.

Pros:

- It's a great way to get your feet wet with selling.
- It's easy to reach out to your immediate network.

- You'll get feedback about your work.

Con:

- You only have so many friends and family, and they only need so many pots.
- Eventually you will have to move on.

Art Fairs and Shows

Over the years I have done many different types of shows and fairs. The most consistent show that I have done is the Art Wander. The Art Wander is a self-guided studio tour in Carver County, MN. I set my wheel up and have many pots for sale; people can watch me demo and hold the finished pieces in their hands. Often the kids will hang out for hours, mesmerized by the wheel throwing. I don't have to travel far for this event, but for many artists, packing up their vehicle and getting pots to an event every weekend, all summer, is how they make their living.

Pros:

- Many people are ready to spend money and browse pottery/art.
- You get face-to-face time with customers.
- People can touch and hold your pottery and see it in real life.
- You have the ability to sell yourself in person.

Cons:

- Traveling to shows can be time-consuming.
- Setup and takedown.
- You lose some creating time.
- Shows can cost a lot of money.

Galleries or Retail

A local gallery has been representing my work for a while now. It's great to be a part of the community and help support the local art shops. I find that online and in the coffeehouse, I can sell many mugs and smaller items. The bigger items like bowls, platters, and specialty items sell better when they are displayed in the gallery. Typically, I get higher prices for the gallery work as well.

Pros:

- If you're selling pots in bulk, the store deals with selling logistics, marketing, and display.
- You can take advantage of the store's existing customers, the right kind of customers.

Cons:

- Stores can take anywhere from 20 to 50 percent of the sale price.
- Getting into galleries can be difficult.

Storefront

This could mean selling out of your own studio or another retail shop that you own.

This is the main place that I have sold my pottery for the last ten years. We have three coffeeshop locations, and all have pottery on the shelves for sale. We have become well known for our mugs, cups, and other functional pieces. It works very well to finish a piece, throw a price on it, and put it on the shelf to wait for it to eventually sell.

Pros:

- You keep all the sales.
- You get face-to-face interactions with customers.
- You get local traffic.
- You are in control.

Cons:

- Setting up a brick-and-mortar shop can be complicated and expensive.
- Opening hours mean you need either to hire employees or take time away from creating to run it.

Online

Over the past two years I have found the biggest opportunity for sales is online. By bringing yourself online, you are opening yourself and your work up to literally billions of people.

Pros:

- Huge market: the entire world become your potential customers.

- You keep close to 100 percent of the profits (credit card fees or other platform fees can cut into this).

- Branding and marketing can be highly effective.

Cons:

- Tons of competition means it can be difficult to stand out.

- Packing and shipping is a huge added cost and time constraint.

- It takes a lot of time to develop the skills required to market yourself and your work (especially photography, video-making, posting, blogging, however you are hoping to be seen by your customers), which means time away from creating.

Different Ways to Sell Online

Website

A great way to sell online is through your own website. This way you can collect your customers' information, set your own rules, and conduct business however you see fit. When you sell on other websites such as Etsy, Amazon, or Kickstarter, you are playing by their rules and trying to sell to their customers. There are many different platforms on which to build a website from Squarespace, Wix, and Shopify to Wordpress and many others. You can also pay a web designer to help you create a site that will share your brand with the world. It can be complicated to set up and run your own website, which is why many artists choose to first sell on sites like Etsy.

Etsy

Etsy is a great way for artists to sell their work. It works well for potters and producers of other handmade, unique items. Posting things for sale is quick and easy, and back-end costs like shipping can be remarkably low.

Kickstarter or Indiegogo

Crowdfunding sites are a great way to build hype and raise money for specific projects. We did a Kickstarter campaign when we were building out our new studio, and it went a long way toward helping us finish the project in a timely and relatively stress-free manner. Many of these crowdfunding sites allow you to take pre-orders. People can choose what they want, and you tailor production specifically to their orders. This way you know things are sold before you actually make them.

Social Media

You can always sell direct to consumers through the different social-media sites, like Instagram, Facebook, Twitter, etc. If people want to purchase an item, you just gather their information, send them their piece, collect payment through sites like PayPal or Venmo (or alternatively by check or through other payment collection services), and BAM you're in business!

Pricing Your Art

When first starting out, figuring out how to price your work can be intimidating and just downright difficult. You look online and see a coffee mug for fourteen dollars, and then you find another artist who is selling a handmade piece for over $140! How can there be a tenfold difference between those pieces?

I have always thought about pricing from two different perspectives. First, supply and demand. Second, making sure you are getting paid what you want for the time you are putting in. I have found that combining both of these methods to find your own personal pricing structure can be a great place to start. Only through pricing and selling your work over a period of time can you grasp what kind of pricing structure you feel comfortable with.

Hourly Rate Method

Making sure that you are getting paid for the time you spend on your pottery is the first thing that goes into pricing. This is an equation I use to figure out a starting price point:

((Hours spent x hourly rate) / number of pieces finished) + (Cost of materials / number of pieces finished) = Price per piece

For example, say you spend twenty hours in the studio each week and are able to produce thirty pieces. Set your hourly rate at a point you would be happy with, so let's say forty dollars per hour.

$$((20 \times \$40) / 30) + \$4.00 = \$30.67 \text{ per pot}$$

You might be able to produce way more than thirty pieces in twenty hours, or way less. Your cost of materials might be way higher or lower than four bucks per pot. Typically, in ceramics and pottery, as long as you are buying larger quantities of clay and glaze and firing full kilns, the actual cost of materials is relatively low. The main cost involved in pottery is the labor and time spent creating.

Supply and Demand

Supply is the amount that you produce. Demand is how interested your customers are in buying your pieces. How these two measurements taken together can go a long way toward setting the price.

For example, a few years ago I came up with an idea I thought would be very popular, the Minnesota mug. It's a mug with a slab cutout in the shape of Minnesota (unglazed to give a rustic feel and look) that I have found Minnesotans love! I thought this idea would be a hit, and at the time I was selling mugs anywhere from fourteen to sixteen dollars. I decided I would make one hundred mugs and release them at twenty dollars apiece, not knowing what would happen. The mugs sold out in less than a day, and I knew that I had a hit! The problem was I knew that to make another hundred mugs would take many weeks or even months! The price had to go up. From there the price went up to twenty-four dollars per mug for a couple years. When I feel like I can't keep up, then I just incrementally start charging more. We are now charging much more than twenty-four dollars, both because demand has stayed high and supply has stayed relatively low (partly due to me being a little sick of making Minnesota Mugs). We have also made many different iterations of the mug. The ones selling now are far superior in quality to the earliest versions.

The Comparison Method

The last thing to consider would be comparing your prices to others' work. Looking around at other ceramic artists and comparing what prices they are charging can be an effective method when looking at your own business model. Keep in mind that time, experience, and trial and error are the best ways to figure out your pricing model.

Using all three of these methods, supply and demand, hourly rate, and comparison, can go a long way to help you figure out a pricing structure that will get you paid while also selling your wonderful pots.

How to Pack and Ship Pottery

Packing and shipping pottery can be stressful and intimidating if you have never done it before. You have pieces that you have carefully crafted from mud to magnificent, and the thought of boxing them up and shipping them can be daunting. One of my first big orders came from Texas for a full dinnerware set. After months of work I was finally ready to ship it. I waited for confirmation to come that the pieces had arrived safely, and, to my horror, almost all of the plates had broken. I was mortified, months of work were wasted, and I came close to saying I would never ship pottery again.

I am happy to say that this year we have successfully packaged and shipped over five hundred pots, all over the world, with zero breakage. The biggest difference between shipping my first ever pots and how I package them now is the two-box, or box-inside-a-box, method.

For a typical eight to twenty-four ounce cup/mug, a six-inch square box inside of a bigger ten-inch square box works well.

Wrap the pot in Bubble Wrap or other cushioning material.

Put the wrapped pot inside the smaller box.

Put a layer of peanuts or packing material in the base of the bigger box.

Put the smaller box and any marketing/promo material inside the box and fill up
with more peanuts or packing material.

Tape up the box and ship it off around the world with total confidence it will
arrive safely.

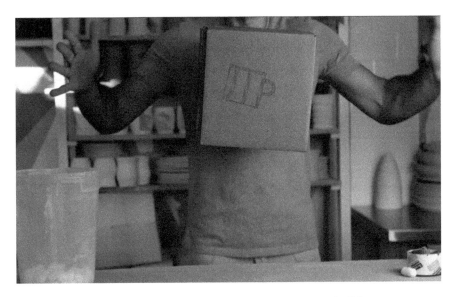

I have tested this method by throwing packages off a two-story building onto a concrete slab, as well as throwing them on the ground as hard as I can, and it holds up to any force.

Conclusion

"You choose your own level of involvement."

—*Fight Club*

You can dive deep into every part of the process or you can choose to let others do the chemistry. Potters can choose to make their own clay, formulate their own glaze recipes, and build and design their own kilns and studios. Alternatively, you can buy clay ready to be crafted, buy glazes that have been formulated and tested, and be a part of a community studio. The more you learn, the more you realize how much more there is to know.

Although I am obsessed with pottery and it is my greatest passion outside of my family, I am an entrepreneur first and a potter second. People often ask me if they should go pursue their passion for pottery full time. I tell them that they shouldn't think about being a full-time potter, they should think about being an entrepreneur. An entrepreneur who creates and sells pottery. The mythical pottery career, spending hours and hours in the studio, is rare. To be successful creating and selling art, one has to spend many hours not creating art, but creating a business. Building business and marketing skills outside of pottery, and combining them with your love and skills in crafting clay, is key to being successful.

Successful artists are successful because they love the journey of creating. Selling and producing pottery to sell is important, but a love of the craft must come first. If you love what you are doing and creating and are committed to putting in work outside of the studio, the sales will come. It is one of the most satisfying things in the world to create functional pieces with your hands that other people want to buy and use in their lives. I encourage everyone to explore their own creativity to create and sell practical pottery.

I have found joy and a love for clay that I want to share. I hope that this book sparks an interest in the endless possibilities of pottery and ceramics and a desire to create a sustainable business around your art. Someone once told me that every space on earth could use ceramics. From decorative vases to dog bowls, cups, wall hangings, sculptures, and many more, any space or task can be enhanced with handmade pottery. I hope that you can find something in this book to enhance your life, just as pottery enhances lives all over the world.

Clay, pottery, and ceramics can be a pursuit that lasts a lifetime. One can spend decades in the medium and still be trying new techniques. I have struggled writing this book because I felt as if there were too many parts of the process that I was leaving out, or too many aspects of the medium that were outside of my expertise. I set out to write an all-encompassing book about pottery, and I realized now that I have fallen short. There are too many techniques and possibilities to be contained in one book. A successful potter must learn to experiment on their own and discover the untapped creativity within themselves. This book was meant to be a guide for those interested in ceramics, but in reality, I think it turned into an inspirational tool to spark interest in the magic of clay. I hope that you can find the same awe and wonder in clay that I have, and that you can experience the joy of taking nothing but a lump of mud and turning it into a piece of functional art that can be used daily

FAQs

How long after you've thrown a pot on the wheel do you flip it over to trim and put a handle on?

This is one of the most common questions I get, and it is a difficult one to answer because it truly depends on the environment in which the pieces are drying. If the space is humid with little or no airflow, the pieces may take over ten hours before they are ready to be handled or trimmed. If the space is dry and has drafts or airflow going, the pieces might be ready to work on in as little as thirty minutes. Each studio space differs in the amount of time it takes clay to dry. It will even change based on the season. Here in Minnesota, the summers are humid, and the winters are very dry. This means that in the summer, pieces may take what seems like forever to dry, while in the wintertime the drying goes much quicker.

How do you prevent s-cracks, cracks from drying, and warping?

S-cracks and warping can be frustrating and can happen for a variety of reasons. I have found that making sure that pieces dry evenly and consistently is the number one thing to prevent these issues. Throwing your pieces so that all parts of the pot are a consistent thickness is key to drying evenly. If a piece is very thick on the base, or if it was thrown before being centered, this can cause uneven thickness and lead to cracks and warping later on in the process. Also make sure that, as it dries, one side is not drying quicker than the other; you may find that certain parts of the studio have drafts that will dry pots unevenly, which can lead to problems. One way to combat these issues is to dry slowly! Drying slowly allows you to control the pace at which all parts of the pots are drying. A damp box is a sealed container which works well for drying pots slowly and evenly. You can also put plastic over pots that you want to dry slower. Pots do not have to be dried slowly as long as they are drying evenly, but drying slowly can help with many of these issues.

Another way to minimize cracking is to make sure that there is not excess water when throwing. Make sure to sop up any excess water or slip before leaving the pot to dry.

What kind of clay do you use?

I spent many years working with a buff stoneware from Continental Clay in Minneapolis, MN. This stoneware has a nice brown color and can be fired from Cone 6 to 10. Recently I have been experimenting with other clays, like a dark iron stoneware and B-Clay or B-Mix, which is a porcelain/stoneware mix with a very soft feel and white color. When deciding on a clay, it is important to understand that every clay has a different range of temperature at which is it vitrified. It is important that your clay reaches its vitrification temperature so that the clay is not porous and will not absorb liquid. I find that it is best to talk with the clay manufacturers about what kind of clay is best for your needs and what kind of work you will be making. When in doubt, I would start with a basic stoneware that is rated to around Cone 6. The desired finish and glaze options also must match the clay you are using. For example, you would not want to use a low-fire glaze rated to Cone 04 on a high-fire clay body that vitrifies at Cone 5.

Do you mix your own glazes?

In college, we were required to mix up glazes and recipes. In my current ceramics journey, mixing and testing my own glazes is a part of the process that I have decided to give over to commercial glaze companies like Mayco. Most people who mix their own glazes follow recipes from other potters. There is a plethora of different recipes that can be found online or in books, and if you can follow a recipe out of a cookbook, you can most likely mix up your own batches of glazes. A book by John Britt, *The Complete Guide to Mid-Range Glazes: Glazing and Firing at Cones 4–7*, is a fantastic way to get started in mixing your own glazes if you are interested. As in all parts of the ceramic process, you can choose your own level of involvement. You can go dig up your own clay and chemicals to make everything necessary, although it is much more efficient from a time and effort standpoint to let others do the clay mixing and glaze testing.

How do you price your pottery?

Pricing your pottery once you are ready to sell can be one of the hardest and most daunting parts of the process. I look at things with three different methods, and then start to experiment after that: hourly rate, supply and demand, and comparison with competitors.

(See page 175 for more on this.)

How do I get started if I don't have a studio?

Look for a shared space, art center, or somewhere that teaches classes. This can be a fantastic way to get your foot in the door and see if this is something that's right for you before spending a lot of time and money setting up your own studio. You can also ask around with local potters and see if they will trade work time for studio time. This is a great way to learn about running a studio and what it is actually like to be a potter. Potters can always use a few extra hands in the studio.

What kind of wheel and kiln should I buy?

When first starting out, looking for a used wheel and kiln can help to bring the cost down. There are a lot of wheels and kilns sitting in basements and garages, put there after someone was sure they were going to get into pottery. The first kiln I ever bought was for two hundred dollars, and I was able to fire it hundreds of times and sell thousands of pots. The next kiln I purchased brand new was over three thousand dollars. I would look for used wheels and kilns in one of the bigger brands. Amaco/Brent, Skutt, and Shimpo are a few that create products that will last years.

What do you wish you knew when you first started?

I wish I knew that in order to make it successfully as a potter who wants to sell their work, a lot of time has to be spent on things other than creating. The time spent on marketing and promoting yourself is as or more important than the time spent working with clay. Every artist's dream is to spend hours and hours in the studio creating, but in reality this is where the term "starving artist" comes from. If you are not working on marketing or developing your online presence or your other business skills, then it will be very difficult to make it as an artist or craftsperson.

Alternatively, I also wish that I would have realized that selling pottery and creating can be a viable and lucrative business. For a long time in my business career I treated pottery and ceramics as a fun little hobby. It made a little money, but not enough to take it seriously. Right before I started my YouTube channel, I decided to really go for it and try to take my pottery and ceramics to the next level, creating a real viable business out of it. I spent many years treating pottery as a hobby, but now I know that creating a real business around pottery is not only very viable, but is also an incredibly rewarding endeavor.

Cone Chart

Cone	Degrees Farenheit
022	1087
021	1112
020	1159
019	1252
018	1319
017	1360
016	1422
015	1456
014	1485
013	1539
012	1582
011	1607
010	1657
09	1688
08	1728
07	1789
06	1828
05	1888
04	1945
03	1987
02	2016
01	2046
1	2079
2	2088
3	2106
4	2124
5	2167
6	2232
7	2262
8	2280
9	2300
10	2345

About the Author

Jon Schmidt is a potter and entrepreneur who owns Mocha Monkey coffeehouses in Minnesota, where everything is served on handmade pottery. Jon is also a well know YouTuber and pottery influencer, creating videos weekly to change the pottery industry. Jon strives to impact the world by inspiring others to live out their dreams and make the world unique, one pot at a time.

CPSIA information can be obtained
at www.ICGtesting.com
Printed in the USA
JSHW071301150223
37784JS00009B/468